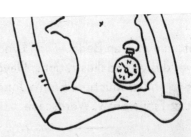

EXTRaordiNaRy
TRaVeLLERS

THE LITTLE MUSEUM

Petit Musée

Written by Karen Beddow & Lyndsay Macaulay

The Little Museum

Written by Karen Beddow and Lyndsay Macaulay
Cover design and illustrations: Daydream Designs
Design and production: Emma Jones, Wordscape
Editor: Fiona Shaw, Wordscape

Printed and bound in Great Britain by Clays Ltd, Elcograf S.p.A.

ISBN: 978-1-8381594-0-5

First published in September 2020 by Mini Travellers

minitravellers.co.uk

For Lily, Isobel, Eve,
Ruby and Beth

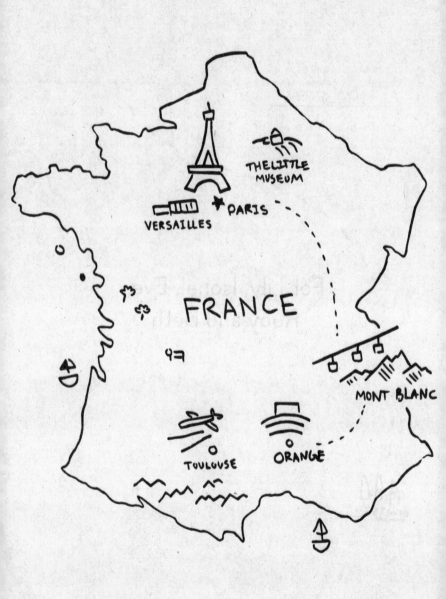

With thanks to my husband Matthew Beddow, without whom there would not be an Extraordinary Travellers series. For his ideas, his early mornings and his creation of Athena right at the very beginning. To my extended family for their comments and their suggestions and their belief we could do it.

It's also thanks to my three crazy Mini Travellers, Lily, Isobel and Eve that my writing journey began when I started Mini Travellers and decided to try life as a freelancer so I could work from home. Before that I was a litigation lawyer worrying about the location of commas and deadlines - I guess not too much has changed.

To Daydream Designs (Sian and Aleyna) for their illustrations and for their patience with us and many changes as we worked out what we wanted. To Wordscape for steering the ship and meeting every crazy deadline we set.

To Emma Green in the early days for believing in the project, Naomi Jones for helping to shape the characters, Clare Corbett for her audio version of the first few chapters which helped bring the book to life, and to Sarah for the Extraordinary name.

With thanks to all those of you who have read this, bought pre-orders without question and loved our idea, dreamt up on a long car journey in Africa a number of years ago.

Finally, with thanks to Lyndsay Macaulay who came on board with the project to bring Extraordinary Travellers to life. She had faith in the idea and the dream and it couldn't have been written without her.

CONTENTS

CONTENTS

Chapter 1

THE BEACH AT THE END OF THE ROad

1924

I t was a sunny day with no clouds in the sky, but Athena's face and lips prickled as the cold wind snapped against her skin. She pulled her black trench coat around her closely to keep out the chill.

Athena Strong lived in a higgledy-piggledy fisherman's cottage in a town by the sea. Her favourite place was the long blonde sandy beach at the end of her road. She could escape the noise of the four brothers and three sisters – and baby Aristotle – Grandpa, two grandmas and Mum and Dad, that she shared a house with there.

She could taste the salt in the air. Waves broke over the shells. The seawater fizzed as it sunk into the sand, washing away the footsteps made by Athena's tall brown boots.

Athena was a scientist and an inventor. To tell you the truth, she was an extra special inventor of incredible things. She collected the flotsam and jetsam* she found washed up on the beach. So far, she had invented a watch that could stop time and a hat that could make you disappear. She was a genius.

Athena looked around to make sure no one was watching her from behind the sand dunes or on the fishing boats out at sea. She was alone.

Under her arm was a large rolled-up piece of paper, a magnifying glass and a compass. She unrolled the paper and stared down at a map of the world.

Athena wanted to travel. Not to the beach at the end of the road. She wanted to see the world.

Athena pointed at a spot on the map and whispered something that no one else could hear.

The map started to glow. A light shone out from the soft paper, casting a rainbow of reflections of the sea across her face.

Athena smiled. It was the smile of someone who knew they had got something right. She gripped the paper so hard that her fingers started to tingle.

Then she closed her eyes and vanished.

* Do you know what flotsam and jetsam are? No, me neither. Athena did. *Flotsam* is the wreckage of sunken ships which is found washed up on the seashore. *Jetsam* is the stuff that's thrown overboard – sometimes to make the boat lighter. You could find amazing stuff on the beach. Athena knew that one person's rubbish was another's treasure. Weirdly, the words flotsam and jetsam are very rarely found apart – they're almost always written together, a bit like fish and chips.

Chapter 2

PARIS IN THE MIDDLE OF THE NIGHT

tonight

The old, rusty, black van drove through Paris with its lights turned off. It was trying hard not to be seen, even though it would soon be three o'clock in the morning and everyone had gone to bed. Even the birds, who like to wake up early, were still asleep.

"Where is it?" The driver sounded anxious.

The driver was a huge French man. He was so tall, he had to squeeze into the van like a snail into a shell. His arms were as thick as your head. He had a long wiry black beard and even longer silky black hair. His name was Jacques.

"Don't worry Jacques, you can't miss it," snapped the passenger. "It's the big tower that looks like the Eiffel Tower. Because it is the Eiffel Tower!"

11

In France, they call it **La Tour Eiffel** and they say it like this: **"LA TOOR EE-FELL"**

The passenger was the complete opposite to Jacques. She was a ten-year-old girl with striking long white hair and piercing clear blue eyes. Her name was Sylvie Argent.

You say her last name like this **"AHH JOHN"**. I bet you know lots of French words. I hope you don't mind me telling you that **argent** is the French word for silver. If Sylvie was at your school, the register would say Sylvie Silver.

"There it is!" Sylvie shouted.

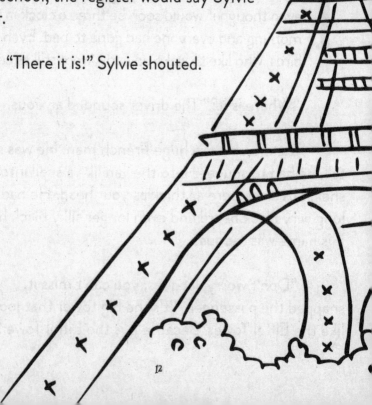

She folded up the map and pointed out of the window. A very big brown tower, with four pillars, criss-cross joists and a point to the top, sat on the other side of the river. The tower was lit with golden yellow lights. Jacques drove the van across a bridge and stopped. Not underneath it. Right in front of it. Sylvie jumped out of the van and ran to the back doors. She threw them open. Jacques was a bit slower getting out the door. He squeezed his head out first, then his thick arms. Finally, his body followed. Jacques was double the height of Sylvie.

"Hurry up Jacques," hissed Sylvie. She was getting impatient.

"Get that box out and put it over there." Sylvie pointed to a patch of grass.

"*Oui Patron*," replied Jacques.

In English, that's "Yes Boss".

Jacques lifted the black box out of the van. It was an old wooden box, the size of four shoe boxes. It was extremely heavy. On the side were three dials and two brass knobs. On the top was a big polished brass funnel, like you find at the end of a trumpet.

Jacques put the box down gently on the grass. Sylvie fiddled with one of the dials on the side of the box. The dial had the letters A and S in the middle. She pointed the arrow to the word 'small'. Next, she turned the trumpet toward the tower.

Sylvie looked down at her watch and waited for the long hand to reach 12. Tick... tick... tick. It was exactly three o'clock in the morning. The lights on the tower began to twinkle and flash. Jacques stared at the sparkling lights reaching high into the sky. He had never seen anything so pretty.

"The lights sparkle every hour through the night," said Sylvie. She winked at Jacques as she pressed the large red button on the top of the box. Nothing happened.

Sylvie didn't like waiting. Usually, people did exactly what she wanted, 'tout de suite'.

That means 'straight away'. You say it like this. **"TOOT SWEET"**. It's one of my favourites. "Mum, can I have a drink? **TOOT SWEET!**"

A whooshing noise started to come from the box. Like an extremely loud vacuum cleaner. Air rushed into the funnel. Sylvie put her hands over her ears. Jacques grabbed his long black beard to stop the funnel sucking it down too. The noise stopped as quickly as it had started.

All of a sudden it was dark. The lights on the tower had been turned off. "What happened?" whispered Jacques.

Sylvie pointed to where the Eiffel Tower had been a moment ago. Jacques followed her outstretched arm. He looked up, back down and finally, up again. The Eiffel Tower had vanished.

"Where's it gone?" gasped Jacques. He couldn't believe his eyes.

She lowered her arm and pointed at what looked like a small Christmas tree, exactly underneath where the tower used to be.

"There it is. The machine has made it smaller." Sylvie looked more pleased than Jacques had ever seen her. "It worked! It worked! It worked!" She jumped up and down.

"Fantastique!" she shouted.

I bet you can guess what that means! There are lots of words in French that are very like the English word. We'll learn more of these later.

"Allez, vite. {ALLAY VEET} Put it in the back of the van and let's get out of here," she commanded.

This means 'hurry up'. Or 'go faster'. Maybe your parents say it when you're putting your coat on before going to school?

The birds in the trees of Paris woke up first, as always. A few hours later, the woman who worked in the shop at the top of the tower parked her car in her usual parking space. She walked to the lift at the bottom of the tower and reached out her hand to press the button.

But there was no button. There was no lift. There was no Eiffel Tower.

Chapter 3

a VERY RaINY day IN ENGLaNd

It was a rainy Saturday at Tom and Lucy's house. Dad was trying to fix his bike. The bike he never used.

Mum was working in her study again. Tom and Lucy were bored. But what they didn't know was that this rainy Saturday was going to be no ordinary day.

Tom was eight years old with thick brown hair. He spent hours making sure his curls were in just the right spot. Naturally cool; done but undone.

Lucy was ten years old. Nothing about her was ever neat or tidy. She had fluffy brown hair with a mind of its own and a fringe that curled up in the rain. Dad said her bedroom was the messiest in the world. But it wasn't to Lucy. She knew exactly where everything should be and today her pencil case was missing. Again.

17

She was cross. Her annoying brother had been into her room again. "Tom. Where are you?" she shouted. "You know I hate it when people go into my room and move stuff around."

"Ssshhh," said Tom. Lucy followed the sound of her brother. It was coming from Mum's study. She translated languages like French and Spanish into English, as well as teaching.

"Tom you can't be in here. Mum will go mad." She was right. There was one big rule in their house: "stay out of Mum's study".

After Lucy's bedroom, Tom thought the study was the messiest room in the world. There were books on the floor. The shelves were all jumbled up and there were half-empty coffee cups everywhere.

"I saw the lights flashing and knocked on the door to check Mum was OK. When I knocked, the door just opened," he whispered. Lucy didn't believe him. "It wasn't my fault!" he said quickly. He was nervous. "Quick, lock the door behind you!"

"How do you and Mum find anything in your rooms?" he asked Lucy, looking around with a frown on his face. "I have no idea how you know when something is missing." He pushed Lucy's pencil case into her hand.

"Thanks," said Lucy. She knew her mum's study wasn't a mess. Lucy knew everything was exactly where her mum wanted it to be.

On the desk sat a framed, faded photograph of a young woman gazing out to sea. You could almost see the wind gusting across the bay, blowing her hair and making the tails of her black trench coat dance.

An old metal watch and an enormous magnifying glass lay next to the photo. The glass head was the size of a dinner plate. Tom picked it up. On the handle were lots of dials like a bike lock, but with letters instead of numbers. There were two gold stars at either end of the letters. The letters lined up between the stars to spell FRANCE.

On the bottom of the handle were the initials
A. S.

Lucy held the watch in her hand but, when she looked closer, she realised it didn't look quite right. It had only one pointer and had the letters N E S and W, on the face instead of numbers. It was a compass. She turned it over. On the back were the same letters, *A* and *S*.

Lucy looked up at the computer. On the screen was a French website. In big letters across the screen were the words *"On a volé la Tour Eiffel."*

"Wow!" said Tom. He was holding the magnifying glass up to the screen. "The Eiffel Tower's gone!"

"What. How do you know that?" snapped Lucy. "You can't read French."

"Are you mad?" said Tom. "It's in English. It says THE EIFFEL TOWER HAS BEEN STOLEN."

Lucy snatched the magnifying glass from him and held it up to the computer. When she put it in front of the screen, all the words changed from French into English.

"That's impossible," she whispered.

"Completely impossible," agreed Tom. Looking through the huge magnifying glass together they read the rest of the page.

Paris woke up this morning to find the world-famous tower was missing. The Eiffel Tower is visited by over seven million people every year. Police say they have no witnesses, and no one has claimed responsibility. The President is understood to be in a meeting with his advisers and will make a comment shortly.

Tom and Lucy looked at each other. They thought the same thing together. This is how Mum learnt to speak so many languages.

"Where is Mum?" wondered Lucy, out loud. As she said the last 'm' of 'Mum', the pointer on the compass started spinning faster and faster. Soon, it just looked like a blur. The pointer started to glow and the lights in the room began flashing. This was no ordinary compass.

Finally, the needle stopped. It was pointing at the gap between Tom and Lucy. They spun round to discover the needle was pointing at their mum. They looked at each other. They looked at the locked door.

Mum had appeared out of nowhere. She was looking down at a large map, lost in her own thoughts. Tom and Lucy were too shocked to speak.

Mum looked up slowly from the map and saw she was back in her study. "Hmm," she said. "Oh dear." She thought for a moment.

"Oh well, I always knew you'd find out sooner or later, once you got older." They'd thought she might be cross but she was quite calm.

"What's going on Mum?" asked Tom, sounding a little scared. But she didn't answer his question.

"Right then." Her faced changed from surprised to one they knew better. She'd made a decision about something. "I'm going to be late for an important meeting, so you two had better come with me."

"What – is – going – on – MUM?" Lucy fixed her mum with a stare.

There was a knock on the door. "Is everything OK Helen?" It was Dad.

"Come in Nick," Mum replied and walked over to unlock the door. She whispered in his ear. "I think it's time," she said. He looked at Tom and Lucy and nodded.

Speaking to them all now, she said, "Someone has found one of Athena's inventions and has just used it in Paris." As she spoke, she pointed to Paris on the map. The lights in the room started to flash again.

"What's happening?" mumbled Tom. "Where are we going?" But before their mum could answer, they were gone.

The half-empty coffee cups and messy shelves were all alone. The woman wearing the black coat in the old picture looked out onto an empty room.

Chapter 4

THE LITTLE MUSEUM

Petit Musée

The rusty old van rattled along the country roads. Jacques had driven through the night. It was now nearly nine o'clock in the morning, but Sylvie was still asleep.

Jacques was hungry. Most French people would have had their croissant, baguette, and coffee by now.

He didn't like to wake up La Patron while she was asleep, but he hadn't eaten anything since they'd left for Paris. The sound of his huge tummy rumbling was so loud it made Sylvie twist in her seat as she slept.

French breakfasts are world famous. I know you might have eaten a croissant and French bread before but, in case you didn't know, this is how you say it properly:

Croissant – QUA-SON

Jus d'orange – JOO D ORANGE

Baguette – BAGG-ET

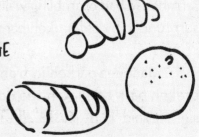

Jacques nudged Sylvie's arm as gently as he could. Which was not very gently at all. Sylvie woke with a start. **"J'ai faim Patron,"** he said.

JAY-FAM, of course, means 'I'm hungry'.

Sylvie had a mean streak sometimes. But you've probably guessed this by now. After all, she's just stolen the Eiffel Tower. "We can't stop now!" she replied with a cross frown. "We'll be home in ten minutes."

Jacques gripped the steering wheel and started to drive faster. "Let's make it five minutes!" They drove down a straight road with tall trees on either side as the early morning sun started to warm the day. He turned down a narrow track.

The van bumped and jumped as Jacques drove towards the farmhouse that was Sylvie's home. The land on their left and right was almost completely flat, and they could see for miles across the open fields. The farmhouse had crumbling walls and tired windows. It was surrounded by old broken barns with tin roofs and walls.

Jacques parked in front of the oldest and most broken barn of all. On the door was a hand painted sign. It said 'Petit Musée'. {PET EE MEWSEE}

That's right – 'Little Museum'. You're getting the hang of this now.

Sylvie's family had been farmers for over 100 years. It was her dad's job now and he worked very hard. Jacques helped her father on the farm. When he wasn't helping steal the Eiffel Tower, that is.

Most of the time Sylvie was left to do what she wanted and most of the time Sylvie thought this was perfect. Sylvie took an old key out of her pocket and put it into the rusty lock on the door of the barn.

She waited with her head down for a moment before going inside. There was just her and Jacques. No one else was there to see her new exhibit. No one else was there to share it with her.

Her mother had died soon after she was born, and Sylvie had no memories of her. There was just one photo on the wall in their house of her mum sitting on an old tractor. Sylvie looked at it nearly every day.

"Put the tower over there," said Sylvie pointing to the corner. The barn was nearly empty. She had asked her father if she could use it for her school project. He said **"Oui"** but did not look up from his magazine about tractors.

Have you worked this one out yet? **Oui**. You say it like **"WE"**. It means 'Yes'.

Jacques placed the Eiffel Tower beneath a hand painted sign reading **'La Tour Eiffel'**. He looked around the dusty barn. Around the walls were more signs above more empty spaces. Sylvie had been busy. He finally understood what the barn was for.

The sign above the empty space next to the tower simply read **'Château de Versailles'**.

Château means 'castle' or 'palace'. We're going to read a lot more about them.

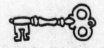

Chapter 5

BONJOUR MONSIEUR LE PRÉSIDENT

L ucy thought she was flying. It was like that moment when she was at the top of the highest jump on her trampoline. It only lasted a second before she felt the floor return underneath her feet. Lucy opened her eyes very slowly.

They were in a large room with a very high ceiling and three windows along one wall. The windows were the tallest that Lucy had ever seen and had heavy gold curtains on either side. Lucy could tell that this was an important room for a very important person.

Next to the enormous desk stacked with papers and folders was a red, white and blue flag. The flag was taller than the man standing next to it. He was wearing an expensive grey suit, white shirt and blue silk tie. Lucy noticed his beautiful blue gemstone cufflinks. Neat, thick brown eyebrows and a furrowed brow framed his deep brown eyes and pointy nose. He looked very serious. Lucy thought he looked like a man with a very big problem.

Mum and Dad turned to Lucy and Tom and smiled as if to say, "Don't worry." Then they walked across the room to greet the serious man. "**Bonjour Monsieur le Président**".

Bonjour means 'hello'. You say it like this: "**BON JOUR**".

Lucy reached out and held Tom's hand. His eyes were still shut tight. "Tom. Open your eyes," she whispered. "You're not going to believe this."

Tom opened his eyes even more slowly than Lucy did. He looked around the room in amazement. This was not Mum's study. It was like a room from a museum they visited on school trips. The sofas and chairs had gold and silver patterns on the cushions. The green carpet was a riot of swirls and flowers. On the walls were mirrors with gold edges. There were LOTS of paintings of people standing around looking at each other.

Above their heads was a chandelier with what looked like a million crystals. The lights twinkled as the sunlight shone through the huge windows.

'Chandelier' is a word that is the same in English and French. Did you know that nearly a third of the words we use come from French? Television is one I bet you know.

The President turned around and looked at Tom and Lucy. "Bonjour les enfants."

This means 'Hello children'. You say it like this: "BON JOR LES ON-FONS".

"Tom. Lucy. Please meet Président Bernhard. He is a special client."

'Client' means someone you help or tell what to do. It's another word that's the same in French and English, by the way.

"Ahh yes. Tom and Lucy. I've heard a lot about you," said the President. "I'm sure you know your mum is a special lady. She tells me this is your first trip with the map."

Tom and Lucy didn't know what to say so they stood there and tried to smile. They looked at the map their mum was still holding in her hand. "Mr President," said Mum. "Do you have any idea who would want to steal the Eiffel Tower?"

"Non. C'est terrible. We have no idea!" exclaimed the President. "How did they do this? C'est très important." The President walked back to his red-topped desk and slumped into his chair.

You see. Two more words that are almost the same. Terrible and important. There really are a lot of them. C'est terrible {SEH TER-EEY-BLE} means 'it's terrible'.

"Mr President. I assure you that knowing how they did this is the easy part," replied Mum. She was using the voice she used when Tom and Lucy asked a silly question.

"Athena invented a lot of incredible things before she disappeared." As she said the name Athena, she glanced at Tom and Lucy before looking back at the President. Her look said, 'listen carefully'.

"One of the inventions we have been trying to find is the sizing funnel." Tom and Lucy could hardly breathe. Their mum was full of surprises.

"Athena was very good at keeping her inventions secret," Mum told the President. "She realised that if her inventions were to fall into the wrong hands, they could be used in the wrong way."

Then she paused. Tom and Lucy could see that Mum was thinking hard. "This is going to be difficult to explain and keep the invention a secret."

She turned to the President. "This may be the League of Extraordinary Travellers' biggest test yet".

"I think it's time for us to go," said Mum, as she started to unroll the map.

Lucy had been keeping quiet as she listened very carefully to everything. But she had so many questions, she felt she was about to burst. Lucy clenched her fists and said in as big a voice as she could, "I'm not moving until you tell me who Athena Strong was?"

Mum looked at the President. He made the slightest shrug with his shoulders and said in a warm voice, "it's a good question. I think your children deserve an answer."

"You're right of course," agreed Mum. "I've started in the middle but now it's time to go back to the beginning. Come on kids, it's time to go home."

"**Au revoir Monsieur**," said Mum as she shook his hand.

'**Au revoir**' {**OH RUHVWAR**} is French for goodbye. You must try to remember this as you'll use it all the time in France.

"**Bon voyage mes amies**," the President replied.

This means 'safe journey, my friends'.

Mum pointed at the map like before and said one simple word, 'home'. And they were gone.

Chapter 6

a FIRE aT THE CHÂTEAU de VERSaILLES

Jacques was trying to keep count. He and
Sylvie had been at the Château de Versailles
for an hour and they must have walked
through 100 rooms already.

The Château de Versailles has over 700 rooms
and 70 staircases. It is one of the most famous places
in France. The palace and gardens cover an area the
size of about 30,000 football pitches. It was the home
of Kings of France for over 200 years.

Sylvie looked around. They were standing in a
small, quiet library. Old wooden bookcases with doors
edged in gold covered every wall. Sylvie loved books.

She didn't like school much – it was boring. She'd always found reading and writing easy and she already knew much more than her science teachers. The library reminded Sylvie of her grandfather's house, which had always been full of books.

He had taught her about science and adventure. A few months ago, just before he died, he'd given Sylvie all of his books. He had also given her the amazing black box with the funnel sticking out of the top. When she asked what it was for, he smiled and said "you're a little girl with a special gift for knowing how things work. I am sure you will figure it out."

They kept on walking. Sylvie was looking for something.

Suddenly she grabbed Jacques' hand. **"C'est ici"** she whispered. "It's behind the guard sitting on that chair."

This means 'it's here'. You say it like this: **"SET EESEE"**

The guard turned the page of the magazine she was reading and squirmed on her chair. It was the end of another long day sitting on the most uncomfortable chair in France.

As she turned the page to her favourite section

about cats, everything went dark. She looked up slowly and put on her special cross face. Her 'stare at children when they were about to touch something' face.

She looked up and up, and up. An enormous man stood in front of her. He was holding the hand of a small girl with long, white hair.

The guard tried to smile. With all the children in the palace trying to touch everything all day, Sylvie thought she probably didn't get a chance to do much smiling. The guard's face looked like she was chewing something very sour like a lemon, rather than smiling.

"Excusez-moi," Sylvie asked in a very shy little voice that she had been practising just for today. Sylvie was brilliant, clever, brave and strong. Not shy. She had been practising a lot. "Où sont les toilettes?"

'Excusez-moi' means 'excuse me'. Just like English, it is a polite way to get someone's attention. You say it like this: "EXCOO SAY MWAR"

You have already guessed that 'toilettes' is the word for toilet, haven't you?

The guard stretched out her arm and pointed to the very end of the huge hall. Sylvie nudged Jacques.

He had been practising too. He looked at his feet and pretended to be embarrassed. "I can't take you to the ladies' toilet," he said. He looked at the guard.

"It's OK little one. I will take you," said the guard. "I need to stretch my legs. Follow me."

"Merci Madame," said Sylvie, as she took the hand of the guard. They walked off down the hall together.

Merci. Now, this is a very good word. I am sure you know this one already but, just in case you don't, it means 'THANK YOU'. You say it like this: **"MARE-SEA"**.

Jacques looked around. Everything was going to plan, just as Sylvie had said it would. He sighed. He'd already walked for what seemed like miles through the endless corridors and rooms of the enormous Château de Versailles. 'Why did these old palaces have to be so big?' he asked himself.

His legs were very tired. He looked at the chair. The chair looked at him. It could see how heavy and large Jacques was. If chairs could move this one would have tried to run away as fast as a zebra from a hungry lion. As Jacques sat down the chair made a loud creaking noise as if it was shouting for help from the other chairs in the room. But it didn't break.

Jacques had to admit the Hall of Mirrors was beautiful. Along one wall was a row of windows that looked out onto a very pretty garden. On the opposite wall windows made of hundreds of mirrors reflected the evening sunset. The ceiling was covered in gold-framed paintings of very important people. Hanging down from the ceiling were lots and lots of chandeliers.

Jacques suddenly remembered that he had a job to do. He reached behind his back and felt around on the wall with his thick fingers.

There was the button. Just where Sylvie had said it would be. It was round and about the size of an apple. He waited for Sylvie to come back and saw her and the guard walking back down the Hall of Mirrors towards him. He held his breath and pressed the button.

An impossibly loud alarm started immediately, and a serious voice began saying, *"Au feu! Sortez immédiatement!"* again and again.

'Feu' is the French word for fire. You say it like this. *"FUH"*.

'Sortez' is the French way of saying "leave" or, as your mum and dad would say, "get out". The word for exit is 'SORTIE' and you will see it on lots of signs.

Lots of things happened at once; people started to run, lights started to flash. Security guards started pushing people out of the doors into the gardens. Jacques got up from his chair carefully and met Sylvie in the middle of the room. She smiled and nodded her head towards the exit. "Let's go to work Jacques," she smiled, a glint in her eye.

"Oui Patron," he replied.

They left the building along with everyone else and ran to their van. It was not rusty and black any more. It was now bright red and had a ladder on the roof. Just like an old fire engine.

Jacques and Sylvie opened the doors of the van and took out the black box with the trumpet on the top.

They watched everyone leave the palace and gather in the gardens. Sylvie hoped that the famous water fountain show would start while people waited to head back in. Once again, she was right. Sylvie just knew how things worked and sometimes how they didn't. The fountains began to shimmer. Jets of water danced as hundreds of different-coloured lights were turned on at the same time. Jacques thought it was beautiful.

On the long lawn in front of the house, a fountain of fire erupted from the grass. Everyone watched. No one looked at the palace that was now behind them.

She pointed the trumpet at the Château de Versailles and pressed the red button. Jacques covered his ears. Once again, the air was sucked into the funnel and then the Château de Versailles began to shrink.

The Little Museum had another exhibit.

"What next Patron?" asked Jacques, once he'd safely stowed the château in the back of the van.

"We're going to the mountains," replied Sylvie. "Mont Blanc. The highest mountain in France."

Chapter 7

AN OLD FAMILY SECRET

Lucy and Tom were back in their mum's study. When the lights stopped flashing, everyone started to speak at once.

Mum folded her arms and waited. And waited.

"And why have you never told us any of this before?" was the last question, before Tom and Lucy finally stopped talking.

"Don't worry, we'll talk about everything in a minute. After I've spoken to your dad, I will tell you what you want to know."

Family meetings were important in Tom and Lucy's house. They didn't happen very often. Usually only when someone had done something particularly bad. Like the time Tom had left the bath running and flooded the house. Or the time when Lucy was playing in the car and accidentally released the handbrake, so it crashed into a wall.

Tom and Lucy sat in silence.

Dad spoke first.

"Your mum and I have agreed that we owe you an explanation. But I'm afraid we won't be able to answer all of your questions, as there is still a lot we don't know either."

Tom and Lucy looked at each other in confusion.

Tom and Lucy's dad was a fun dad most of the time. As far as Tom and Lucy knew, he worked as a nurse in the local hospital. Lucy thought his job must be stressful as he liked to play so many games with them. He was trying to become a magician at the moment to make his patients smile. But, as usual, he had bought lots of stuff to practise with and not used it very often. The truth is, he was rubbish at magic tricks.

"Your mum's family are good at keeping secrets," their dad said. He turned to Tom and Lucy and raised an eyebrow.

Their mum took over. "One day when I was visiting your grandad, I was searching in the attic for some books that had been packed away. At the very back of the attic was an old chest I'd never seen before."

This was getting interesting, thought Lucy. She stared at her mum and was afraid to blink in case she missed something.

"It was like a pirate's chest. Painted on the top of it were the words 'The League of Extraordinary Travellers'. But it had a big, old lock on the front."

"Did you have the key?" asked Tom anxiously. He was getting impatient now. He needed the world to be lined up straight and instead it was becoming more confusing, more jumbled.

"Don't worry Tom," said Dad. "We'll get to that".

Mum continued: "before your Grandma Lysandra died, she gave me a key and told me to keep it safe. She said I would need it one day."

Mum pulled on the long chain she always wore around her neck and showed them the old key hanging from it. The key was smooth from years of handling, with a series of intricate grooves. Lucy reached out her hand and held the key. She wanted to know everything. Lucy was different to Tom. She liked jumbled and confusing. She was much happier with riddles and mysteries than her brother was. This was brilliant.

Their mum continued: "Inside was the map, compass and magnifying glass, with the photo of a woman in tall brown boots. And a folder with lots of scraps of paper and letters."

Their dad put the folder on the kitchen table. "You'll have plenty of time to look through all this later," he said.

"There was also a letter from your Grandma Lysandra to me." She had the tiniest tear in the corner of her eye. Tom didn't notice, but Lucy did.

She read out the letter.

Dear Hera, she started.

"But that's not your name, Mum," said Tom. "It's Helen". This was another thing that was different to how it was supposed to be. This was one of the biggest surprises of all.

"I'm sorry Tom." She held his hand. "Only a few people who know about Athena call me by that name." She continued to read out the letter...

Dear Hera,

Your great grandmother was called Athena. She was a truly remarkable person. I had hoped to tell you all about her, but I don't know if I'll get the chance. Athena was a scientist and an inventor of extra special things. But more than anything, she wanted to help people.

Much of what Athena invented was lost in the terrible fire at our home before she disappeared. Some of the inventions that survived are in this chest. There are also other inventions of Athena's around the world. Some she left with special people and some were stolen or lost.

Our family decided to try to find all of Athena's inventions and to make sure they weren't being used for harm. Now I must pass this task to you, and one day, on to your children. The map will help you get to where you want to go. The magnifying glass will help you interpret unknown words. The compass will help you find your way.

With some old friends of Athena and some very important people around the world, we set up the League of Extraordinary Travellers.

Hera, will you help to continue the work of the League of Extraordinary Travellers?

With love, Mother.

She put the letter carefully back into the envelope. Dad spoke next.

"You see, your mum and I like to say we're Extraordinary Travellers with a very special job. You've already met one other member of the League of Extraordinary Travellers..."

"Have we?" asked Tom.

"Of course we have, Tom," said Lucy helpfully. "The President of France. Right Dad?"

"Yes, that's right Lucy." He paused and took out another piece of paper from the folder. It was a list of names.

He looked at Mum. She smiled a lovely big smile and nodded. "So..." He paused for a few moments. "Tom and Lucy, would you like to become the newest members of the League of Extraordinary Travellers?"

"YES!" they shouted together.

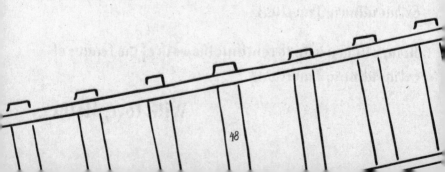

Chapter 8

MOUNTAIN HIGH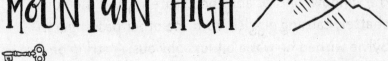

T he rhythm of the train speeding across the countryside offered a moment of quiet for Sylvie. Soft lavender fields, mirror lakes and dense rich forests whizzed past. Industrial towns and local markets flashed past the windows as they sped to their target. The Alps would be their biggest challenge so far. Could they really steal Mont Blanc from under the noses of France, Italy and Switzerland? It was the highest mountain in Europe, after all.

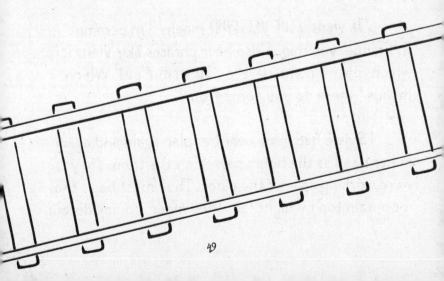

Jacques dozed noisily in the corner of the carriage. His bulk tucked into the gap between the seat and the table and his cheek squashed flat against the window. Snores and snorts interrupted the quiet chatter, causing giggles from the other passengers. Sylvie wished he was a bit less obvious. A string of dribble teased at the corner of his mouth. But without him, she knew she couldn't drag her precious box from the train. Let alone succeed in her most epic theft yet...

After what felt like a lifetime, the train made its slow approach to Chamonix Station. Sylvie had been wishing they were already there for the last two hours. She stretched, then scrambled to her feet. She gave Jacques a sharp kick under the table. "Wake up, we're here." Jacques groaned, wiped the drool from his lips and squeezed his stomach free from the table edge. "OK, OK, I'm coming, *je viens*."

'Je viens' {ZHE VEE-ENS} means 'I'm coming'. In France, you might also hear phrases like *'Viens ici'* which means 'come here' or *'Tu viens d'où?'* Which means 'where do you come from?'

Sylvie had gone over her plan again and again in her head as the hours passed on the train. They were working against the clock. They must be at the mountain top by night fall. They made a quick detour to pick up mountain bikes, before dashing to the Aiguille du Midi cable car station. It would whisk them to their final stop before the summit.

The Aiguille du Midi (AG-WEE DU MEEDEE) cable car station is very famous – you may even spot it in *The World is Not Enough*, a James Bond film. 'Aiguillle du Midi' means 'noon needle' in English, which is a pretty interesting description.

Sylvie and Jacques stepped onto the final cable car of the day. The doors closed behind them and Sylvie breathed a sigh of relief as it pulled out into the open valley. The weight of Jacques added an uncomfortable tilt to the movement, as the car dangled from its cable. The view of the rugged mountain peak ahead was crystal clear. People looked like dots, miles below. The snow and ice of the glacier glistened. Stealing the mountain would be better than any diamond ring. It would be the perfect exhibit for her project.

The rumbling of Jacques' stomach rolled like thunder. It jolted Sylvie back from her thoughts. At least there was a restaurant at the top, she remembered. It would be a great place to stay warm and kill some time before it got dark. **"Tartiflette?"** she asked Jacques, which brought a broad smile to his face. Even she couldn't resist the creamy, cheesy, bacon-ey, potato-ey speciality of the region. **C'est délicieux! {SE DAYLEESEEUH}**

Proper mountain food was what they needed for the long night ahead.

It can be really fun to learn about food in different places. You can practise talking about foods you like by saying **J'aime... "ZHEM"**

La fromage {LA FROM AZH} – cheese

La pomme de terre {LA POMM DUH TAIR} – potato

Le bacon {LUH BAY CUN} – bacon

And foods you don't like by saying **"Je n'aime pas..."** – **"JUH NEM PAAH"**

Have you noticed that some of the words for foods are the same in French as in English?

Bon appétit {BUN APP-EY-TEET} – enjoy your meal!

As they finished their second helping, they noticed the restaurant was emptying. Visitors were heading home. "Not long now," said Sylvie. "Let's find somewhere to hide until it gets really dark.

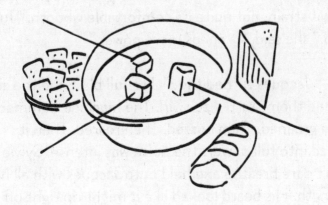

From their hiding spot, Sylvie and Jacques watched the cable car take passengers back to town. An eerie quiet crept around them as they waited impatiently to be sure they would not be seen. Sylvie didn't want to leave it too long as they might get stuck – or worse – frozen on the mountain. But she couldn't risk being interrupted.

"Now," said Sylvie, "let's do it now." Jacques unpacked the black box from its blanket and fiddled with the dials. "Okay, you're sure we're ready, *sommes-nous prêts?*" {SOM NOOS PREHS}

They had never tried to shrink something so big. But Sylvie was eager to bring this treasure back to her collection. "We're ready," she confirmed with a small nod.

Jacques turned on the machine. It came to life slowly with the familiar creaks and groans. Sylvie could hear it strain, not quite its comfortable whoosh. "Turn it up," she said, "it needs more power."

Jacques turned the dial to full blast and the air around them started to swirl. The machine hummed. Then groaned. Then buzzed. Then roared. Then it kicked into full power. The noise was intense. Sylvie didn't dare breathe and held onto Jacques with all her strength. His beard looked like it might rip right off his face. She couldn't tell if they would be dragged into the funnel, or if the machine might just explode. Maybe the mountain was too much for it. But, like a snake swallowing an antelope, suddenly, it was done. They had shrunk Mont Blanc, the mountain peak. In the distance was the sparkling rock, a mix of ice and drama, ready to add to her display.

Sylvie and Jacques scooped up the machine and raced back to their mountain bikes. They strapped the black box to the back, clipped on their helmets and headlights and set off down the ski route. Thank goodness it was only a blue route!

Now the race was on, Sylvie and Jacques dashed to collect their prize in the remaining moonlight. Sylvie knew they didn't have long. The machine had taken way longer to shrink Mont Blanc than the Eiffel Tower. They could not be caught in the act on the mountain side at dawn. Thankfully, the moon stayed low and the sun was slow to rise. Sylvie and Jacques, exhausted, had made it safely away with their trophy.

All that was left to do was post it home to the farm. Perched on a bench beside the road, Sylvie packed Mont Blanc into a box with layers and layers of bubble wrap. She didn't want her prize to get broken on its journey back across France. Plus, it would be fun to pop the bubbles later. She labelled it with her name and address in big, confident letters. Then she combed the wind from her hair and headed across the road into Chamonix post office.

The woman at the counter didn't look up from her crossword as she weighed the parcel and added the right stamps. Sylvie thanked her, a smile creeping across her face. No one will think to look for a mountain at the post office, a job well done.

You might want to send a postcard from France. Postcards and stamps can be bought in a number of places such as at newsagents **(le Tabac)**. You would then go to **La Poste**, the post office, to mail your postcards.

She skipped quickly out of the post office and crossed the road to where Jacques was waiting with the bikes. The town was beginning to stir. Shops were opening and cafés setting out chairs for the day ahead. It was definitely time for them to go.

The street was eager with cyclists ready for a long day in lycra and hikers wrapped up for the climb ahead. On the corner, Sylvie noticed a family talking excitedly. She watched for a moment as the boy checked his hair in the window of a shop. The girl stopped talking for a moment and met her gaze. 'British tourists', she thought to herself – not knowing that she was looking at Tom and Lucy with their mum and dad.

The cloud sat low in the sky, waiting for the morning sun to burn it away. No one had yet noticed something missing in the distance. But still, Sylvie sensed that they had not gone completely unnoticed. The hairs on the back of her neck bristled. She couldn't quite place the feeling, but someone, somewhere was watching them.

Chapter 9

AN EXTRAORDINARY MEETING OF THE LEAGUE OF EXTRAORDINARY TRAVELLERS

The room fell silent. In the distance, Tom and Lucy could hear the whirling blades of the helicopter. The Chief of Police and Monsieur le Président were about to join them.

"As soon as they land, we can get the meeting started," said Dad. The League of Extraordinary Travellers had gathered for an emergency meeting at the scene of the latest crime. Tom and Lucy waited nervously with Mum and Dad to hear about the latest drama.

"This is a catastrophe. We have no time to lose," exclaimed Monsieur le Président. "Now, someone has stolen Mont Blanc – what next? We are under attack. We must find the sizing funnel and fast. The world is starting to ask questions. First, the Eiffel Tower. Now this. We can't keep this a secret for much longer."

Lucy glanced at Tom across the room with a look that said 'We need to get out of here fast and start looking for clues.'

Hera stepped forward and started to explain more about the sizing funnel. "Monsieur le Président, we know the sizing funnel must be nearby. It can only shrink something as big as Mont Blanc from 100 metres away. The thieves must still be in the area. If we work fast, we can find them before they get too far."

The Chief of Police nodded as Mum spoke. "We have our best forensic team looking for evidence. We have closed the airports and the borders with Italy and Switzerland. We cannot let the thieves get away this time."

At that moment, a mobile phone rang. The room waited on tenterhooks to hear what the Chief of Police had to say. She looked calm and in control, her uniform super crisp and not a strand of her thick black hair out of place.

"Monsieur le Président, my team has looked at the security cameras. We have a lead. At 4pm yesterday a tall male with a black curly beard and a small girl with long, white hair were spotted. They got onto the last cable car with bikes and a large black item wrapped in blankets. They were later seen by a waiter, having a meal of tartiflette, but then disappeared. They did not get on the cable car to return down the mountain. So either they got lost on the mountain overnight or travelled home a different way. It is very unlikely that a child would survive a stay on the mountain overnight."

At that moment, the Chief of Police's phone pinged. Her team had forwarded a photo of the man and girl getting onto the cable car. The League of Extraordinary Travellers looked stunned. Who is this man and what is he doing with this poor young girl?

Lucy looked at the photo closely. There was something about the girl that seemed strangely familiar. Had she seen her somewhere before?

Mum took the phone from the Chief of Police. "Amazing work Colette," she said. "This will help us find the thief and return the missing items. We need to rescue that poor girl; she might be in danger." She reached into her pocket for the compass and unpacked the map from her rucksack. She lay the map on the table and placed the compass on top.

"This is no time for map reading," Tom thought to himself. "We need to get out there and look for the thieves and rescue the girl." But, just then, Mum started to describe the man in the picture to the compass.

Il a les yeux noisette: **"EEL A LAYS YUH NWAZETT"** – "He's got hazel eyes"
Il a les cheveux noirs et raides: **"EEL A LAY SHUVUH NWAR AY RED"** – "He has black, straight hair"
Il est grand: **"EEL EH GRAND"** – "He's tall"
Il est large: **"EEL EHST LARDGJ"** – "He's broad"

If you want to talk about how you look in French, you would say "J'ai..." – **ZHAY** – "I have..."

As she talked, the arrow on the compass began to spin. But it just kept on spinning. "It isn't working," said Mum, annoyed. "We need the name of the thief to be able to find him. We must find out more."

"Unless," said Lucy, "the compass can't take us anywhere because the thief is still here? Maybe they are nearby?"

Chapter 10

a PLaNE To catCH

S ylvie couldn't quite shake the feeling of being watched. But each treasure she collected made her want more. It was time to move fast and think differently if she was to complete her project without being detected.

With Mont Blanc on its way to the farm, Sylvie and Jacques headed south-west. 'We need somewhere quiet to lie low,' Sylvie thought to herself. She was spooked that someone might be on to her, watching and waiting for her next move.

The train journey to Toulouse was long and boring. Jacques tried his best to keep her entertained. But I Spy, Yellow Car and Twenty Questions only seemed to make time move slower. Sylvie was fast running out of interest in trains. She needed something to help complete

her project. "If I had my own plane," she exclaimed, "we could collect treasures and trophies from across the world. Let's go to Toulouse! They build the largest plane in the world in Toulouse. That would give me plenty of room to bring my collection home. I need my own Airbus A380."

Jacques looked worried. He always stroked his black beard when he worried. Stealing a mountain was one thing. Stealing a tower quite another, because they didn't actually belong to anyone. And no one was trying to make sure they didn't get in or out. Stealing an aeroplane – from a top-secret aeroplane factory – needed one clever plan.

Luckily, Sylvie was already on to it. "It's simple," she said. "They might expect a person to try to break into their manufacturing plant. But they definitely wouldn't expect a tiny mouse-sized human to steal an aeroplane."

"But where will we find a tiny mouse-sized human?" asked Jacques, looking confused.

"Right here," said Sylvie. "We'll point the sizing funnel at you. You can creep in undetected, cut through the alarms, open the door and let me in. No one will suspect a thing." She looked very pleased with her idea. Jacques did not. He liked being tall. His mother called him 'her strapping boy'. Seeing the doubtful look on his face, Sylvie reassured him, "I'll set the funnel for five minutes. You'll be back to normal in no time at all. Trust me."

As night fell in Toulouse, Sylvie and Jacques waited nervously to put their plan into action. "Don't forget, you have just five minutes to get in through the vent, cut the alarms and open the door for me. You'd better not get distracted or the guards will spot you," Sylvie said, but she knew Jacques wouldn't let her down.

She pointed the sizing funnel at him, set the size dial to 'maximum' and the timer to five minutes. This time, he let himself be sucked in the direction of the swirling winds. Before they both knew it, he was no more than 10 centimetres high. "Boom, it worked," she shouted, "now get in there quick and open the door before it wears off." Jacques crept off in the direction of a factory vent. 'Don't mess this up,' Sylvie thought to herself as she looked nervously at the countdown on her phone. Two minutes and counting. One minute and counting.

Inside, Jacques was racing through an air conditioning vent. Sylvie had found the factory plans online. Third left, second right, go forward for 100 paces. He tried to keep Sylvie's instructions clear in his head and ignore the ticking of his watch urging him to go faster. 'Focus,' he told himself over and over, 'Don't let Le Patron down now.'

With 15 seconds to spare, Sylvie heard footsteps. With her heart in her mouth, she braced herself ready to run. The door opened. Jacques had done it; he'd actually made it. 'Yes, we're in!' Sylvie thought. But there was no time to lose now. They had a plane to shrink.

"Je dois prendre l'avion" [ZHE DWE PREND-R LAVVYEN] is how you would say "I have a plane to catch" in French.

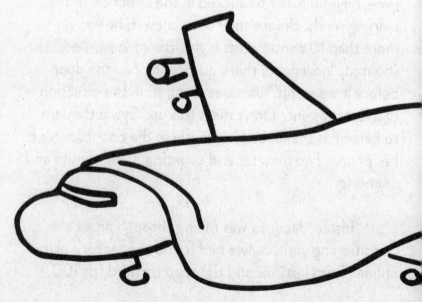

They bundled the sizing funnel inside the hangar. Sylvie took a last glance around to see if there were any passing guards. She set the dials and directed it at a brand new Airbus A380. A gust of air, a swirl of dust and the perfect, beautiful wonder of technology was the size of a paper aeroplane.

Sylvie and Jacques held their breath as they waited to see if the noise had caught the attention of the guards. They heard footsteps in the distance. "Are they headed this way?" Jacques whispered. Sylvie peeked through a slit in the door. "Don't move!" she hissed, waiting to see if the guard would spot the missing plane.

"Phew, he's gone. Right, let's get out of here quick," said Sylvie. "Better wrap it in that sheet so we don't break it on the way out. The last thing we want is a new plane with a broken wing."

Jacques packed up the plane and sat it on top of the special black box. They made a fast exit into the dark night as the security guards played Snap and drank tea in the break room.

But Sylvie and Jacques hadn't gone un-noticed by everyone. Watching in the shadows was a woman. She had seen them leave the factory with a large black box and what looked like a toy aeroplane wrapped in an old sheet.

The woman, dressed in a long black trench coat, followed Sylvie and Jacques. She ducked elegantly in and out of the shadows like a spy, staying close enough to hear their excited chatter.

Sylvie and Jacques made it to the station with minutes to spare for the train to Orange.

In French, it's pronounced: **"ORANZH."**

They dashed on board, relieved that they had made their escape from the factory. And that they were both back to their usual size.

The woman watched, listening for the announcer to say where the train was heading.

"Mesdames, messieurs, bonjour. La SNCF et votre Chef de Bord vous souhaitent la bienvenue dans ce TGV à destination d'Orange."

This means 'Hello, ladies and gentlemen. SNCF and your train manager welcome you to this TGV train bound for Orange.' We would normally tell you how this sounds, but all train announcements are a bit of a blur. {MAY DAMS, MAY SURES, BON JOUR, LA ESS EN CEE EFF, something, something, something, ORANZH}

As the train pulled out of the station, the woman watched Sylvie and Jacques through the window of the train. She took out her mobile phone, dialled a number and spoke quietly.

"Be ready. They're on their way to the Roman amphitheatre in Orange," she said in a soft English accent that sounded like the sea.

As Sylvie stared out of the train window, relieved to be on the move, she spotted a woman in a black coat and brown boots watching from the platform. She felt the same chill spread over her as she had in Chamonix.

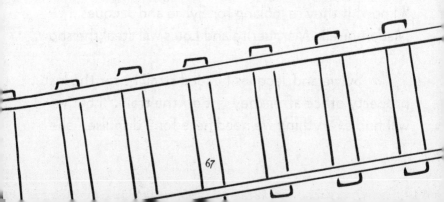

Chapter 11

To Steal The Show

"Jacques, did you see her? You must have seen her. The tall woman, wearing the long black coat?" Sylvie asked anxiously. But of course, Jacques hadn't seen anyone. She decided not to worry about it right now. They were safely on the train, racing to their next destination. No one could possibly know where they were heading now. Sylvie kept one eye on the plane-shaped package above their heads. The other on the old, battered sizing funnel box in the luggage compartment beside them.

She spent the journey hatching a new plan. 'If someone is watching us...' she thought for a minute. 'I know! If they're looking for Sylvie and Jacques... Mademoiselle Marguerite and Louis will steal the show.'

Sylvie and Jacques headed straight for the lost property office after they got off the train. "I bet we will find everything we need here for a disguise," she explained to Jacques. After a quick rummage, their transformations took shape. Sylvie scraped back her long white hair, wriggled into a frilly white shirt and blue velvet coat. She added a dirty old beret and drew on some brown eyebrows and a moustache. An old empty black violin case finished the look.

Finding a costume for Jacques was more challenging. He squeezed his huge arms and broad stomach into a statuesque gold ballgown. He gasped as Sylvie laced the ribbons at the back. A dusty white wig covered his black curls. 'Hmm, the beard,' thought Sylvie, spotting a beautiful black lacy fan in the corner. "Well, that should do it," she said.

Jacques thought himself quite the picture. He fanned himself and giggled at his reflection in the mirror. "Stop preening and get a move on," Sylvie snapped.

Orange was packed with visitors for the famous opera festival. The streets bustled with people dashing from concerto to recital, and buying tickets for a showing of *Carmen*.

The amphitheatre was a glorious sight. The imposing theatre wall, the cascading seats, marble friezes, statues. Sylvie couldn't help but be a little bit impressed that soon this too would be at home in her barn.

It was strange to think that 195cm Mademoiselle Marguerite blended in amongst the opera lovers. But, thankfully, they looked like part of the show. In fact, Jacques was enjoying posing for selfies with some of the tourists a little too much for Sylvie's liking.

Following the tip off, Lucy, Tom, Mum and Dad had travelled to Orange. They took their seats for the performance of *Carmen* and watched for anything out of the ordinary. Lucy scanned the audience with her opera glasses. Even in a crowd this big, surely, she could spot the unlikely pair of thieves.

The opera was magical. She'd never seen anything like it before in her life. Soaring voices. Radiant costumes. The drama, the elegance, the music of the orchestra. Lucy was mesmerised. The performance ended all too quickly. With tears in her eyes, Lucy realised that they hadn't spotted the thieves. "We've missed them," she said, frustrated. "And now they're going to get away with stealing the amphitheatre."

"Not yet," said Mum. "Outside the amphitheatre is a team of undercover police. You and Tom need to head to the van and help them watch for any suspicious behaviour. Dad and I are going inside for a closer look. We'll meet you back at the van."

Lucy and Tom joined the police team. They put their headphones on and watched the security cameras. Mum and Dad headed behind the basilicae to a secret side door.

"The finest wall in my kingdom," is how Louis XIV described the Roman amphitheatre in Orange. It is 103 metres long, with walls 1.80 metres thick and 37 metres high. The outside is divided into three levels – the first has three doors which open out onto the stage. The basilicae are beautiful towers positioned on each side of the stage.

Once inside, Mum and Dad searched the dressing rooms for anyone fitting Sylvie and Jacques' description. In the distance, through a cloud of old hairspray they saw an unlikely pair still in full costume. "Suspicious," said Mum. "Looks like we might be onto something after all."

Ducking behind a massive pillar of flowers, Mum and Dad watched as the curious pair started to unpack. The old wooden box caught Mum's eye. "The sizing funnel – that's it! We need to get to it before they shrink anything else!"

Dad jumped up, knocking over the pillar with a clatter. Petals flew everywhere.

Hearing the crash, Sylvie checked behind her. Out of the corner of her eye, running away from the chaos, she spotted the British tourists from Chamonix. 'I knew we were being watched. Well, I'm not leaving here without the amphitheatre, so I guess they're coming with me,' she decided.

Tom and Lucy also heard the crash blast through their headphones. The camera zoomed in on a tall mademoiselle and a young boy with a suspicious, smudged moustache. "Oh no, they were in disguise," cried Tom. "That's why we missed them in the audience."

"Look, there's Mum and Dad. They're running straight towards them. They need backup, let's go Tom," shouted Lucy, throwing down her headphones and leaping out of the van. Lucy and Tom sprinted to the door of the theatre and dashed to where the strange couple were hiding.

But Lucy and Tom were not the only ones to have seen Mum and Dad. Sylvie saw them running towards her and Jacques. Scanning the room for a plan, she spotted an old paper coffee cup. "Got it!" she said. She flipped the dial on the sizing funnel in the opposite direction. Aiming at the cup, she transformed it into a huge container, filling the whole corridor. Before Mum and Dad could stop, they ran straight into the cup. Sylvie turned the dial back down to shrink and fired a blast at the cup. Back to its original size, Sylvie scooped up the cup and put the lid on tight with Mum and Dad, now tiny, inside.

Lucy and Tom saw the flash and heard the intense noise of the funnel as Mum and Dad disappeared from view.

"Jacques, we need to get out of here super-fast," barked Sylvie, "Let's go!"

"But what about the amphitheatre?" cried Jacques.

"Just leave it, we need to go. Grab the sizing funnel and the plane," Sylvie said. "I can hear police sirens."

Sylvie and Jacques gathered their things and burst through the side door. They dashed towards the train station. "The police are getting closer," Jacques panted, pushing his wig out of his eyes. "I'm not sure we're going to get away in time."

"Just you watch," whispered Sylvie, dragging Jacques into a dark doorway. She quickly unpacked the sizing funnel, set the dial to grow, and blasted it at a park bench. With a whoosh, the bench filled the street with the police safely blocked behind it. "Phew, we're safe at last," she panted, patting the lid of the coffee cup still containing the British tourists.

Chapter 12

MISSING MUM and dad

Suddenly, the theatre went quiet. Lucy and Tom realised they were alone. Mum and Dad had vanished, along with the thieves.

"We've lost them," Lucy worried. "What do we do now?"

As a tear ran down her cheek, Tom took her hand. "We'll find them Lucy; you're great at riddles. This is just a really tricky one."

Tom and Lucy checked the room for clues, finding only an empty violin case, a dirty sheet, and a used train ticket. "This doesn't tell us anything we didn't already know," moaned Lucy. "Let's head back to the van and see if the League of Extraordinary Travellers know any more."

Lucy and Tom trudged back to the team waiting outside. "Let's get to a hotel for a good night's sleep" said the Chief of Police, who'd arrived on the scene. "We'll have a better chance of finding them in the morning."

Lucy tossed and turned all night. There had to be something she hadn't thought of. She woke early the next morning feeling like she had barely slept. Tom was awake and making the bed quietly at the other side of the room. "Better get dressed, there might be more news this morning," he said.

Lucy climbed into her crumpled clothes from the day before. "How does Tom always look so pristine?" she thought to herself. Just then she felt a bulge in one of her pockets and put in her hand to see what it was. "The compass," she exclaimed. "That's how we find Mum and Dad."

"Have you still got the map, Tom?" she asked.

"Sure, it's in my rucksack," he said, reaching beside the bed. "What are you thinking?"

"Watch," she said.

Lucy placed the compass onto the map. "Mum and Dad," she said.

The needle of the compass started to spin, and the reassuring rainbow of colour shone from the map over the hotel room.

"It's working," she gasped. Two golden dots appeared on the map, "they're here, look, just outside Paris. We've found them, and maybe we've found the thieves too."

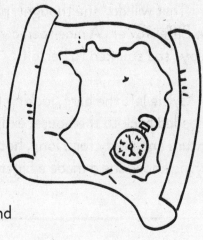

In a barn, just outside Paris, Sylvie breathed a sigh of relief. "Well, that didn't go quite as planned. But at least we made it out without getting caught. And I did bring home something to add to my collection."

Mum and Dad were still trapped in the coffee cup. Sylvie gave them some scraps of left-over **pain au chocolat {PAN O SHOCOLAH}** to keep them going till lunch. She popped the lid back on the coffee cup, checking it was nice and tight and looked around the barn for a safe place to put them.

'That will do,' she thought, placing the cup on top of the Eiffel Tower. 'A nice scenic view of Paris for them to enjoy,' she smirked to herself.

Sylvie left the barn, locking the door behind her. She headed back to the house, exhausted from her adventure and ready for a long, hot shower. But, little did Sylvie know, she'd made a big mistake.

L ucy and Tom joined hands nervously, ready for the compass to take them to Mum and Dad. The needle began to spin, there was a flash of light, and Lucy and Tom felt themselves leave the ground for a split second.

Moments later, they opened their eyes. As the room around them became clear, they realised that they were now in some kind of barn. They could hear chickens in the background and smell the fresh straw on the ground beneath them. As they looked closer, they saw that the barn didn't have the usual things, like cows and tractors. On one side was a miniature Mont Blanc, on the other a miniature Château de Versailles.

In the corner was a tiny Eiffel Tower. And balanced precariously on top, was a paper coffee cup.

Lucy and Tom rushed to the cup. Lifting the lid, they saw Mum and Dad safely sitting inside – if a little bit tiny.

"Oh Mum," said Lucy, "what do we do now? You're mini, you're not even the size of my hands!"

Leaning close to the cup to listen, Lucy and Tom heard Dad whisper, "Don't worry guys. Mum, as always, had an awesome plan. She knew you would use the compass to find us. You are so smart."

Mum and Dad climbed onto Tom's palm and he carefully showed them around the barn.

"Look at this place, it's like a museum of the wonders of France. So many amazing treasures. But why are they all here?" asked Lucy.

Mum pointed further down the barn. Tom carried her over for a closer look. On one side, there was a gap ready for a new exhibit. A fresh sign had been painted in dribbly red letters and was hanging from a nail above a space in the straw. "Le Tour de France," it read.

Chapter 13

a CLOSER LOOK

 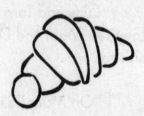

"That's it, the Tour de France cycling race must be their next target," squeaked Mum. "They won't get away with it this time."

Lucy still looked worried. She didn't dare say it out loud, but what on earth were they going to do with a tiny Mum and Dad? They couldn't possibly stop the thieves now. They might not even make it out of the barn.

But Mum had a glint in her eye. Lucy could tell she had an idea.

"This is perfect," Mum said. "We can sneak around without being spotted. We just need to wriggle through that gap in the bottom of the door. Then we'll have a hunt around and find out as much as we can about the thieves. Something tells me the young girl is not as innocent as we first thought."

Dad told Lucy and Tom to stay hidden in the barn and wait for them to come back. If they had any chance of being discovered, they were to use the map and compass to escape to safety.

Tom nodded.

Mum and Dad hugged Lucy's thumb and kissed Tom on the tip of his nose. They squeezed through the gap under the barn door and took off on their mission to find out more.

The farmyard was bright in the morning sun. In the distance they could hear a cow gently mooing and a chicken scratching about, making contented clucking noises.

Did you know that animals in France sound different, too?

Pigs say *"groin groin"*

Ducks say *"coin coin"*

Donkeys say "hi han"

Sheep say "bêê"

Chickens say "cot cot codet"

Cows say "meuh"

"La vache meugle" means "the cow moos" in French.

Across the yard was a slightly scruffy farmhouse. Once-grand blue shutters framed the tired, old windows and thick vine leaves grew over the entire side of the crumbling building. Pots of herbs and banks of lavender scented the warm air. At the back of the house flapped a washing line, a string of off-white socks and underpants wafting in the warm breeze.

"Let's head around the back," said Mum. "It will be much easier to sneak in the back door."

Mum and Dad made a quick dash across the yard, spotting a moment too late the fat farm cat stretched out on a sunny window ledge.

"Don't make a sound," said Mum, throwing a pebble to distract the cat from where they were standing. "Quick, there's the back door. Run!"

Mum and Dad ran as fast as they could. The cat, excited by this new game, made a dash behind them. Mum and Dad raced on and made it to the back door of the farmhouse just in time. Mum crouched to give Dad a bunk up to reach the flap. The cat was getting closer. Mum was sure she could smell the tuna the cat had eaten for breakfast.

Luckily for them, the cat flap swung open easily and Dad pulled Mum up. Together they clambered through into the kitchen, locking the flap to the cat behind them.

The kitchen floor was made of warm terracotta tiles that had not been scrubbed often enough. To one side was a big, old, wooden oak table with a random collection of chairs. On the table was a fresh baguette, a bottle of milk, a bowl of fresh eggs, a chunk of white cheese and a sticky looking jar of apricot jam. "Easily room to seat seven or eight people," said Mum. "I wonder who lives here."

Mum and Dad ventured through the kitchen into the hallway. There was a big staircase leading to bedrooms upstairs. On the wall was a collection of family photos in dusty frames. Dad spotted a picture of the girl with white hair, "Look, there she is," he said, "and again here as a baby. Sylvie Argent, born in March 2010. She must live here. But I don't see the man with the black hair."

In French, they might say "née en mars 2010" –
{NAY ON MARS}

Les mois, French months:

Janvier {ZHANVEEYAY} – January

Février {FAYUREEYAY} – February

Mars {MARSS} – March

Avril {AVREEL} – April

Mai {MAY} – May

Juin {ZHOOANG} – June

Juillet {ZHWEEYAY} – July

Août {OOT} – August

Septembre {SEPTAHMBR} – September

Octobre {OCTOHBR} – October

Novembre {NOVAHMBR} – November

Décembre {DAYSAHMBR} – December

Mum was still silent. On the wall, just above her head, was a picture of a grand looking gentleman, dressed in a striped dark suit with a neatly combed moustache. He had a stiff look on his face, like a head teacher giving out detentions. Next to the man stood a woman. Not just any woman, Athena Strong.

"We need to get back to the League of Extraordinary Travellers right away and tell them what we've found," she said. "Maybe they'll know how the thieves are connected to Athena, and why they're using her inventions."

Mum and Dad met Tom and Lucy back in the barn. "No time to lose, we need to go" said Mum. "We'll fill you in on everything when we get back to the League of Extraordinary Travellers."

Tom and Lucy gathered up the rucksack and the map and headed out of the barn to where they could lay it out flat. Lucy took out the compass and was about to say Monsieur le Président when Tom grabbed her arm.

"Wait, look," said Tom, "over there, on the door of the barn. There's a sign. It looks like the paint is still wet so it must be brand new, what does it say? Ça dit quoi? {SA DEE KWA}

"Le Petit Musée – for my Grandfather and Mother who never got to take me to these places."

"But what does it mean?" asked Lucy. "Another riddle to figure out when we get back to the League of Extraordinary Travellers."

Chapter 14

THE RACE IS ON

"Monsieur le Président," said tiny Mum, standing on the President's desk, "we have so much to tell you.

"We discovered where the thieves are keeping the stolen treasures. They have created a little museum in an old barn just outside Paris.

"And we know their next move – they're going to steal the Tour de France."

Tom looked puzzled, "what's the Tour de France?" he asked.

"The Tour de France is the most famous and most difficult cycling race in the world. It lasts 23 days, covers 3,200 kilometres and has over 200 competitors," replied Monsieur le Président.

"But there is more," said Mum. "The thieves knew Athena Strong. There is a photo of her in their house. We don't know how or why, but she was there in a picture with a mystery man on the farm. That must be how they have her sizing funnel."

"Incredible work team," said Monsieur le Président. "Lucy and Tom, you are doing a fantastic job. I am so glad you are the newest recruits of the League of Extraordinary Travellers." He paused for a moment, then said, "But what do we do now?"

He turned to the Chief of Police. "We will need all of your best officers Colette, to save the Tour de France."

Colette picked up her phone and started to make arrangements.

Mum waved to Lucy. "I have an idea how we can catch the thieves in the act. But we need to pick up something first. Let's make a quick detour home."

'Detour' is another word that is used in both French and English – both mean 'to go a way that's not the shortest route'.

Lucy took out her compass and, in a heartbeat, they were back in Mum's study at home. "Lucy, we need my umbrella, over there, beside the desk. Yes, the one with AS on the side," shouted Mum with her tiny voice. "Right, let's get back to Paris."

Colette, the Chief of Police, had been busy. She had organised one of her strongest policemen to go undercover as a cyclist in the race. He would be a domestique and hide in the group supporting the yellow jersey. A domestique is a very special member of a cycle racing team who assists the team leader to win (often at the expense of his or her own performance). Monsieur le Président looked pleased.

"But how will we keep an eye on them on the ground?" he asked. "We need to stay close to the competitors."

"We will join a marshal on the back of a motorbike," said Mum.

"I can do that," said Lucy.

"OK," said Mum. "Tom, we need you on the radio with the League of Extraordinary Travellers. We will definitely need backup."

Lucy popped Mum and Dad into the pocket of her jacket, checked her helmet was correctly fastened and climbed on the back of the marshal's motorbike. She held on tight to the back of his leathers with one hand and clung onto the open umbrella from Mum's office with the other.

Instantly the motorbike vanished. The umbrella was another one of Athena Strong's amazing inventions. Lucy wondered what other wonderful things she might have created.

Meanwhile, in Paris, Jacques had parked the van in a side street off the main stretch of the race. He opened the rear doors of the van and unfolded a ramp leading to the road. Sylvie was on top of the van where she had set up the sizing funnel pointed in the direction of the open road.

Inside the van below she could hear Jacques muttering crossly as he squeezed his thick arms into a tight police officer's uniform. He tucked his long mirror-like black hair into a police hat and donned a pair of sunglasses and white gloves, then folded himself out the van.

"Tuck your shirt in," barked Sylvie.

"Yes, of course, I'm sorry, je suis desolé {ZHE SWEE DAY-SO-LAY} Patron," replied Jacques, stepping out into the middle of the road. He was in position.

Sylvie gave him a thumbs up. 'Now we wait,' she thought.

Chapter 15

A VOICE FROM NOWHERE

The crowd was cheering, whistling and whooping as the riders of the Tour de France turned the corner.

This is what you might hear if you were standing on the side of the road watching the racers of the Tour de France passing by.

"Allez, allez, allez" – {ALAY, ALAY, ALAY} – go, go, go!
"Vas-y" – {VASEE} – go you!
"Bien joué" – {BEE-EN ZHUYAY} – good job!
"Tu peux le faire" – {T P LEFAYRE} – you can make it!

Heads down, the cyclists were whizzing along the smooth Paris roads like a swarm of colourful bees. Helicopters hovered above recording the scenes for the rest of the world to enjoy on TV later that day.

Up ahead, a single policeman stepped into the middle of the road. The peloton, a fancy name for the pack of cyclists, understood it must be a change in route.

Tucked deep into the pack, Gabriel, the undercover policeman, was pedaling hard. He couldn't quite believe his luck. He was riding in the Tour de France alongside, well – behind actually – his hero, Chris Froome. He saw the policeman redirecting the cyclists. He knew right away that something was wrong. Picking up his radio, he made an emergency call to the League of Extraordinary Travellers.

You might have heard people say "Mayday" when they're in trouble. "Mayday" started as an international distress call in 1923. It was the idea of Frederick Mockford, who was a senior radio officer at Croydon Airport in London. He came up with the idea for 'mayday' because it sounded like the French word *"m'aider"*, which means 'help me'.

Lucy heard Gabriel's urgent transmission and gave the signal to the marshal to go faster. "We need to get ahead of the peloton before they're all shrunk for the Little Museum."

"Allez-allez!" she shouted.

The marshal pressed hard on the throttle and the motorbike kicked up a gear. Lucy felt the air blast on her face. But could they make it in time to save the cyclists?

The front of the pack turned the corner giving cheerful waves and thanks to Jacques for directing them so well.

Sylvie's plan was working. Perched on the roof of the van she quickly thrust the sizing funnel into action. With a loud whoosh, the cyclists started to shrink and disappear into the back of the van.

Holding on like her life depended on it, Lucy and the marshal raced towards where the policeman was waiting. She spotted an alleyway on the right. "Quick, that way," she directed the marshal. "We'll cut them off up ahead."

Leaning into the tight curve, Lucy held her breath, hoping that Mum and Dad were still safely tucked inside her pocket. The motorbike raced down the alleyway, past rubbish bags and through dirty puddles. Still invisible, they scared the life out of a stray dog who was casually helping himself to yesterday's leftovers.

At the end of the alleyway, Lucy and the marshal turned onto the side-road behind Sylvie, who was still waiting on top of the van. They could hear Sylvie laughing excitedly as the tiny cyclists clattered into the back of the van.

The marshal's bike crept up to the front of the van and Lucy hopped off the back. Holding onto the umbrella to stay hidden, she inched closer to get a better look.

She peered through the window. 'Maybe I could pull a wire loose?' Lucy thought, 'but which one?'

Then something glinted in the sunshine catching her eye; the keys to the van!

Quelle chance {KELL SHONCE} – which means 'how lucky!'

Lucy opened the door as quietly as she could. She reached in and pulled the keys from the ignition. "Got them, they'll not be making a speedy get a way now!" she chuckled.

Sylvie heard police sirens. "We'd better get out of here," she shouted and started to pack up the sizing funnel.

Tom and the police were approaching fast. Jacques waved thinking that his disguise would protect him, not realising that in fact they were coming for him and the van. He was now surrounded. "Sylvie, le Patron, quick, go," he shouted.

With the keys safely in her other pocket, Lucy carefully climbed on to the top of the van where Sylvie was hurriedly gathering up the sizing funnel.

"Not so fast," said a voice from nowhere.

Sylvie looked up puzzled. "Who's there?" she demanded, picking up the sizing funnel.

"You're coming with us," said Lucy bravely. "You have some serious explaining to do."

Lucy grabbed Sylvie's hand. She held the umbrella over the unlikely pair making them both invisible to the surrounding police.

"She's vanished," shouted Tom to the police. "And where is Lucy with Mum and Dad?"

Chapter 16

THE FINAL EXHIBIT

*O*pening her eyes, Sylvie realised that she was back in the barn.

"What just happened?" she asked. "Where is Jacques?"

Lucy put down the umbrella, appearing to Sylvie. "You're not the only one who has an Athena Strong invention. But now it's my turn to ask the questions."

Lucy took Mum and Dad out of her pocket and placed them carefully on the top of Mont Blanc.

"Maybe we should start at the beginning," said Lucy. "Who are you?"

Sylvie looked huffily at Lucy. "My name is Sylvie Argent. I am ten years old. I live here on the farm."

"We're the same age," said Lucy.

Sylvie glanced a smile at Lucy.

"How did you get the sizing funnel? And why did you shrink all these things?" asked Lucy.

"Well," said Sylvie. "A few months ago, my grandfather died. He was my best friend. He was the only person who understood me." Sylvie sniffed a little. She was not going to show Lucy that this made her feel sad.

"He gave me all of his books to help remember him. He also left me this box. He said I would figure it out as I'm good at knowing how things work. At first, I didn't know what to do with it. It looks like a piece of junk and I was a bit cross that it wasn't something special. Just a made-up story. Until I accidentally shrank my bike when I was playing with the dials. Then I knew it was interesting. I started to practise using it around the farm. I could make things small and then big again which was pretty cool."

"What do you mean, a 'made-up story'?" asked Lucy.

"My grandfather told me a story of an inventor; a woman called Athena Strong. He wouldn't tell me who she was or why he knew her, only that she was incredible. He said that if I worked hard, I might be an inventor like her. I thought he was just trying to make me more interested in school. It all sounded like a fairy tale. But then he gave me a picture. Here, I'll show you."

Sylvie pulled open a battered old tin box. In the box was a pile of old photos. They had started to curl up at the edges and some had creases and coffee cup rings on them. Sylvie rifled through the pictures until she came to one of Athena Strong. "Look," she said. "This is Athena Strong. That's when I realised that there was a picture of Athena and my grandfather in the hall of our house. So I knew it must be real."

"I suppose you want me to make your parents back to normal again," Sylvie said with a small frown across her face.

"I think that's a good idea," said Lucy.

Lucy smiled at Mum. Maybe Sylvie could be a friend after all.

Sylvie set up the sizing funnel, flicked the dial round and pointed it at Mum and Dad. "Actually, better move them off the top of Mont Blanc just in case I make that full size too," she chuckled.

The funnel groaned and whirred and in a flash Mum and Dad were back to normal size.

"Phew" said Dad, stretching his legs to check everything was still working properly.

Suddenly, the familiar sound of whirring helicopter blades could be heard outside. "What's that?" asked Sylvie, looking worried. "I guess I'm in big trouble."

"You are in big trouble, young lady," said Monsieur le Président, as he walked into the barn.

Sylvie gasped. "Monsieur le Président! Is it really you?"

"It most definitely is. You have caused a great deal of worry. I hope you can explain. We have your accomplice in custody, so you'd better tell me the truth," he said.

Sylvie sat down onto an upturned bucket and started to explain. She told the President everything. Even that Jacques had just helped her out.

The President was shocked. A ten-year-old girl could cause this much trouble?!

Sylvie looked truly sorry as she explained. "Are you going to send me to jail?" she asked, looking at the President.

Monsieur le Président thought for a minute. "I have something much worse in mind for you, young lady, **jeune femme. {ZHEN FEM}** You are clearly a criminal mastermind," he said. "We could do with some more brilliant minds, so it's time to turn your attention and focus to doing good. You are going back to school. It is decided."

Sylvie wasn't sure whether to be relieved or not. Jail or school? Both sounded like terrible options. "What about Jacques? It really wasn't his fault," she trembled.

The Chief of Police stepped forward. "Actually, Monsieur le Président, Jacques showed some excellent skills directing traffic. I think he could be a valuable member of my team."

"That is decided too," said the President. "Jacques will be a traffic officer."

"Now, Sylvie, let's pack up the museum. We will take my helicopter and put everything back where it belongs for all the people to enjoy. France would not be the same without these important landmarks and beautiful works of art. They really are the crème de la crème."

You might have heard the term crème de la crème before. It is used in both French and English. It literally means the cream of the cream – which really means the very best of the best.

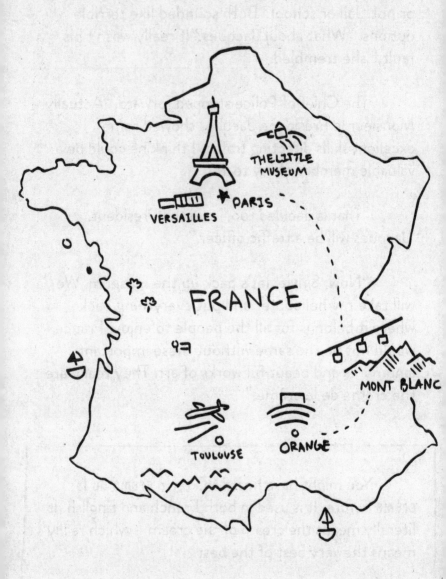

Chapter 17

NEW BEGINNINGS

The day had finally come. Sylvie was starting back at school. She had folded herself awkwardly into her newly-pressed uniform. A stiff blue shirt, plaid pinafore and red bow around her neck. Long red socks with bows at the top and shiny black shoes pressed her toes. She had plaited her long white hair into a neat braid. 'At least I look the part,' she thought.

The bell rang. Sylvie followed the other girls into her new classroom and looked around for a free desk near an open window at the back. 'Perhaps jail was a better option,' she thought to herself.

Quiet fell over the class and the girls hustled to find their seats. At the front stood her new teacher. Tall and elegant, she took off her long black coat and hung it on a peg by the whiteboard.

In scratchy letters she wrote on the board, "Bonjour le class, je m'appelle (JUH MAPPELL), my name is Mademoiselle Athena Strong."

Sylvie watched as her new teacher turned to face the class. In a lilting seashore English accent, she said "S'asseoir les filles, (SA-SAY-WAH LAY FEE) – sit down girls."

Sylvie gasped and looked up. The new teacher gave her a knowing nod.

*A*t the same time in Britain, Tom was struggling with a magic trick in the garden. Scattered across the grass was a spread of cards, dice and a slightly bent magic wand. Lucy made the tricks look effortless while Tom battled to find a toy rabbit in the bottom of Dad's old magician's hat.

Did you know that the father of modern magic was actually French? Jean Eugene Robert-Houdin was born in 1805. He was famous for tricks like the marvellous orange tree and the ethereal suspension. He also started the fashion of wearing top hats. In fact, the Great Houdini was named in respect for Robert-Houdin.

"Perhaps we should stick to real magic adventures," Tom said. "At least we are good at solving them."

Lucy laughed, "We're definitely the best new recruits to the League of Extraordinary Travellers." Dad laughed too, scooping up Tom and Lucy into a big hug.

Mum, who had been working hard in her study all morning, called out into the garden. "Quick everyone, come in here, you need to hear this."

Lucy looked at Mum, who was clutching the map, compass and umbrella in her hand. Her heart skipped a beat. 'Could it be time for another adventure,' she thought.

Lucy and Tom rushed into the lounge. A breaking news report had flashed across the television screen.

Coming live to you from Barcelona, Spain, we have breaking news. The Cathedral of the Holy Cross and Saint Eulalia is floating above the city…

WANT a GLIMPSE of THE NEXT LEAGUE of EXTRAORDINARY TRAVELLERS STORY?

1924

Athena paused.

She could feel the bustle. The air smelt different, warmer, almost closer. So different to her sleepy seaside town.

She slowly opened her eyes to take in her new surroundings. A beautiful wide, elegant tree-lined avenue was filled with busy people rushing to and fro. In the background a market seller yelled her wares for the day. Beautiful, grand women hushed neat children out of the way of men in dark suits and bowler hats, as horse drawn carriages cantered past.

Her wish had become reality. Athena wanted to travel. She loved her hometown but she needed to see the world. And with her invention, she realised, she could. Just minutes ago she was watching the tide roll out over the long blonde beach at the end of her road. The world was now her oyster.

She rolled up the map, packed her compass and magnifying glass safely back into her satchel. Just saying the word 'Barcelona' to her map had brought her here. La Rambla was a hive of activity in the heart of Barcelona. The boulevard spilled over with artists, street performers and building works. A city at the start of something magical. She trembled with excitement.

The busy street seemed so modern, so very cosmopolitan. Athena felt excited. She felt inspired. She glanced around at the pristine windows of cafés steamed with hot coffee and shops selling the latest essentials. She pressed her face up against a shop window to get a closer look. On a bed of soft red velvet lay a row of beautiful wrist watches. Glamorous women's watches with small sparkling faces and gold bracelets, men's watches with strong black leather straps and strict; shining clock faces. Athena couldn't look away. She could feel she was at the edge of a new idea.

It was time for a new adventure.

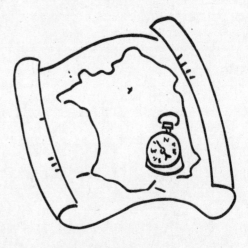

**For more ideas, resources, language and travel tips,
head to minitravellers.co.uk/extraordinary-travellers**